TABLE OF CONTENTS

INTRODUCTION

It all began on 17 December 1903. Orville and Wilbur Wright, brothers and best friends, were at Kitty Hawk, North Carolina, in the United States of America. They were ready to test the Flyer. With Orville at the controls, the Flyer lifted shakily off the ground under its own motor power and flew for twelve seconds. Wilbur took his turn next, soaring above the sand dunes.

The Wright brothers had built and flown the world's first aeroplane. Their invention has transformed the way we travel around the world.

This is their story.

1 GROWING UP

Wilbur Wright was born on 16 April 1867. His brother, Orville, was born on 19 August 1871. Wilbur and Orville had two older brothers called Reuchlin and Lorin and a younger sister called Katharine.

Their mother, Susan Wright, taught her children how to use tools and fix things. They also learned how to cook and sew.

Their father, Milton Wright, was a minister in the United Brethren Church. He kept detailed records about his work and his family. Bishop Wright expected his children to work hard, believe in themselves and find a purpose in life. Going to school was important, but he felt that ten months of school each year was too long. Orville, Wilbur and Katharine were allowed to miss a day or two of school to work on a project or read a book at home. The Wright house was filled with books.

Oil lamps lit the Wrights' house in Dayton, Ohio. There was a pump for water outside the kitchen door and an outhouse at the rear of the house.

When Orville was seven and Wilbur was eleven, their father gave them a toy helicopter. It was made of wood and paper and powered by a rubber band. Wilbur and Orville wound up the rubber band, and the tiny helicopter skittered into the air.

Orville and Wilbur built new and better helicopter models. Orville even fiddled with one at school. He told his teacher that he was making a flying machine. He might even build one big enough for him to fly in!

Eight-year-old Orville was a prankster who bubbled with ideas.

Twelve-year-old Wilbur was a popular athlete and an excellent student.

Wilbur tagged along with Reuchlin and Lorin and their friends. Sometimes Orville and Katharine trailed after Wilbur. Wilbur teased Orville and Katharine.

In the summer the fields around Dayton were perfect for ball games and hide-and-seek. During the winter, Wilbur and his friends played shinny, a kind of ice hockey. Wilbur enjoyed history and geography in school. He was clever and liked living in his own world of ideas.

Will (BACK ROW, CENTRE), Lorin (FRONT ROW, RIGHT), and Reuchlin (BACK ROW, 2ND FROM LEFT) were in a club called Ten Dayton Boys.

Orville liked to tinker with things – to take them apart and put them back together again. He was eager to build kites, after Wilbur showed him how. Orville sold his kites to his friends.

They were teenagers when their mother became ill with tuberculosis. She was weak and needed lots of care. Nineteen-year-old Wilbur stepped in. He took care of his mother for three years, until her death in 1889. Her death was a terrible blow to them all, but especially to Wilbur.

Orville had decided to drop out of school and started a printing business. With Wilbur's help, he made a printing press out of a tombstone, carriage parts and other recycled odds and ends. He published a weekly newsletter, the *West Side News.* Wilbur became the editor. When it failed, the brothers formed Wright & Wright, Job Printers. They printed business cards, posters, flyers and advertisements for local businesses.

Orville's friend Ed Sines works at the printing business.

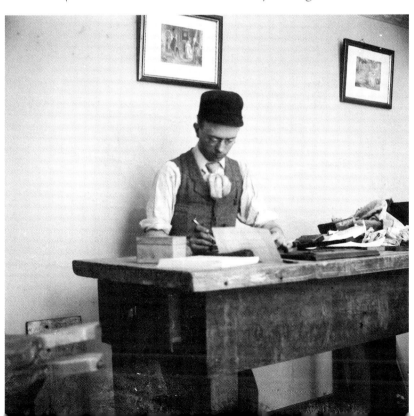

In 1892 Orville and Wilbur both bought a bicycle. Wilbur rode out in the countryside around Dayton. Orville raced other cyclists on a track. Whenever a bicycle broke, the brothers fixed it. They even repaired their friends' bicycles. Before long, they were known as skilled mechanics.

Bored with the printing business, the brothers wanted to try something new. Wilbur, who was twenty-five, and Orville, age twenty-one, opened a bicycle shop.

THE HISTORY OF THE BICYCLE

The bicycle was invented in the early 1800s. A rider sat between two wooden wheels, pushing the bicycle with his feet. Next came the velocipede, or penny farthing, with pedals attached to the large front wheel. The rider might sit as high as one and a half metres off the ground. The safety bicycle, invented in 1885, had chain-driven wheels of equal size and brakes. Cycling became a national craze. By 1886 about a million bicycles had been sold in the United States.

2 FROM BICYCLES TO GLIDERS

Wilbur and Orville 'lived together, played together, worked together, and in fact, thought together'. They even shared a bank account. Working side-by-side in the bicycle shop, they often whistled or hummed the same tune.

Orville wore a large apron over his suit. He didn't want to get dirty. He loved to take things apart to see how they worked. It was just as much fun to put everything back together again.

Dreamy Wilbur ignored the mess on the floor and the smells of glue and oil. Katharine had to remind Wilbur to wash before meals and make sure his clothes were clean.

Wilbur, hard at work in the Wright Cycle shop in 1897.

Wilbur and Orville adored Lorin's children, (LEFT TO RIGHT) *Milton, Leontine and Ivonette.*

The three of them lived at home with their father. Reuchlin and his family lived in Kansas, but Lorin and his family lived nearby. Orville and Wilbur read stories to their nieces and nephews. They made sweets together and put on puppet shows. Orville played his mandolin and Wilbur played his harmonica. They also loved to play with their nieces' and nephews' toys. 'They had a habit of playing with them until they were broken, then repairing them so that they were better than when they were bought,' one niece said.

Both brothers kept up with world news. They read about men flying in balloons and ornithopters, machines with flapping wings. Most readers laughed at the stories, but not Wilbur and Orville.

Otto Lilienthal was testing gliders in Germany. Gliders had no motors. They soared with the wind. Lilienthal would race downhill until the glider's wings swept him off the ground.

After many successful flights, Lilienthal died in a glider crash in 1896. Wilbur wondered what had gone wrong. Was the glider too heavy? Didn't Lilienthal have enough control over his flight?

Wilbur wrote to the Smithsonian Institution in Washington, DC. 'I believe that simple flight . . . is possible to man. I am an enthusiast but not a crank.' He wanted to know more. The Smithsonian sent some information.

Samuel Pierpont Langley, the secretary of the Smithsonian, was testing a flying machine he called an Aerodrome. His remote-controlled model had two pairs of curved wings, a steam engine and a pair of propellers. It had flown for nearly a kilometre until it had run out of steam.

TO FLY LIKE THE BIRDS

From the beginning of time, artists had sketched people and machines with bird-like wings of wood, fabric or feathers. In 1783, French brothers Joseph and Etienne Montgolfier sent up a painted fabric hot-air balloon over Versailles. The passengers were a sheep, a duck and a cockerel. All three animals returned to Earth unharmed.

Wilbur also wrote to Octave Chanute, a retired engineer who had tested gliders on the shores of Lake Michigan. Chanute wrote back to encourage the Wright brothers.

Both brothers watched birds in flight. They agreed that if birds could fly, people should be able to fly in a machine with wings. However, they disagreed about how birds controlled their flight. When they disagreed about something, they could argue for hours.

Octave Chanute's glider had wings mounted on rubber springs. That way, the wings could rock back and forth with the wind.

Orville and his friend Ed Sines repair bicycles in the cycle shop.

"'Tis,' Wilbur would say, "'Tis not,' Orville would argue. In the middle of an argument, they'd often switch sides.

One day in the bicycle shop, Wilbur was twisting a long, narrow, inner tube box. When one end went up, the other went down. All of a sudden, the bent box reminded him of how birds moved their wing tips in the wind. What if he and Orville could work out a way for a pilot to control the bend in the wings of a glider?

The brothers made a glider that could fly like a bird. When one wing tip tilted up, the other tilted down, and the glider turned.

In the bicycle shop, Orville and Wilbur constructed a glider. It was one and a half metres long and was made of wood, wire and cloth. The wing tips were connected. When the brothers made one wing tip tilt up, the other wing tip would tilt down.

Wilbur picked a windy day to test their model. He flew the glider like a kite by tossing it into the wind. Then using cords running from the wings to sticks he held, the glider climbed and dived on command. It was a huge success!

Wilbur and Orville were eager to build something bigger. It had to be strong enough to hold a person. They also needed a testing place with lots of steady wind and open space.

Wilbur wrote to the US Weather Bureau in Washington, DC, asking for a list of the windiest weather stations. The brothers picked a place where the wind blew fifteen to thirty kilometres per hour. It was a tiny fishing village called Kitty Hawk, on the Outer Banks of North Carolina.

EYES ON THE SKY

Wilbur brought the glider parts to Kitty Hawk in September 1900 by train and boat. At Kitty Hawk, there were kilometres of soft sand for flying and landing, and there wouldn't be many onlookers to bother them.

Orville followed a few weeks later. The brothers pitched a tent in the sand and finished putting their glider together.

They soon discovered that the Weather Bureau had given them the *average* wind speed. The wind could gust up to ninety-five kilometres per hour. They tied their tent to a tree, just to be safe. Orville wrote to Katharine: 'When we crawl out of the tent to fix things outside, the sand fairly blinds us. We came down here for wind and sand, and have got them.'

The brothers still flew their glider like a kite. They controlled it with hand-held lines. After days of testing, they decided it would work with a pilot on board.

The Wright brothers' tent at Kitty Hawk was buffeted by wind and sand.

Lying face down on the lower wing, Wilbur flies the glider.

Orville, Wilbur and Bill Tate, the Kitty
Hawk postmaster, hauled the glider to the
top of a sand dune. Wilbur lay face down
on the lower wing. Orville and Bill each
grabbed a wing tip and ran into the wind.
Wilbur yelled, 'Let go!' For a few seconds,
the glider rode the breezes above the sand.
Wilbur made about a dozen flights that day.
In all, he spent two minutes in the air.

By late October, it was time to fold up
the tent and go home. The Wright brothers
still had a bicycle shop to run. However,
they left Kitty Hawk with plenty of ideas.

The following year, the brothers brought a new glider to Kitty Hawk. Much to their disappointment, the 1901 glider was hard to fly, even in the strong winds. They wondered if it had something to do with the curve of the wings.

Wilbur (LEFT) and Orville (RIGHT) test the 1901 glider. This model was much more dangerous than the 1900 glider.

Wilbur and Orville went home much earlier than planned. They went straight to work. All winter long, they tested wing shapes. The brothers wrote down everything in notebooks. This information helped them put together a new glider. They hoped it would be much better.

TESTING WINGS

To test how wings worked, the Wright brothers built a wind tunnel. The wind tunnel was a box — 0.4 metres square and 1.8 metres long — with a fan at one end. They made about two hundred pairs of tiny wings called airfoils. The airfoils were made of metal. They were thin or thick, curved or flat.

The fan blew steady air through the tunnel. Each wing was tested in the tunnel to see how it reacted to moving air. After hundreds of tests, Wilbur and Orville discovered which kind of wing shape would make their glider fly best.

Orville crashes the 1902 glider.

Wilbur and Orville returned to Kitty
Hawk in September 1902. For the first time,
Orville flew. He warped, or bent, the wing
tips to turn left or right. He controlled up
and down movements by the forward
rudder, or elevator. Then Orville crashed.
Luckily, he walked away without a single
injury, but the glider had to be repaired.
Orville wondered what had gone wrong.

During one sleepless night, Orville
worked out a possible solution. What if the
glider's tail could move like a bird's tail?

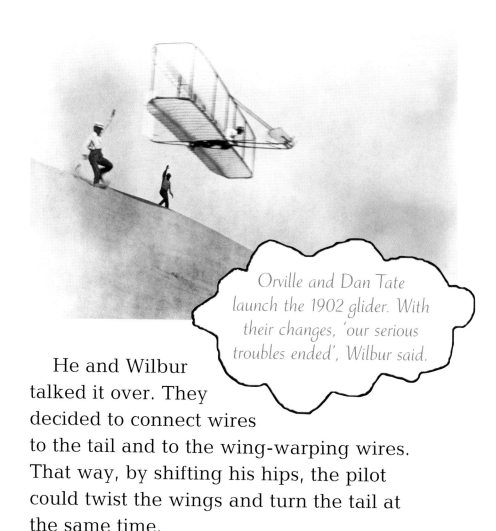

Orville and Dan Tate launch the 1902 glider. With their changes, 'our serious troubles ended', Wilbur said.

He and Wilbur talked it over. They decided to connect wires to the tail and to the wing-warping wires. That way, by shifting his hips, the pilot could twist the wings and turn the tail at the same time.

It worked. When the wind reached about fifty kilometres an hour, the remodelled glider soared over the sand. 'That was the highest wind a gliding machine was ever in, so that we now hold all the records!' Orville wrote.

They had gone over 170 metres, and they had spent twenty-six seconds in the air. Orville and Wilbur had learned how to control flight.

Their 1902 glider flew, but it didn't have an engine. It couldn't take off under its own power and it would never fly very far. However, the brothers were already at work designing an engine. The engine would power propellers that would push the plane into the air. Then they could take off and fly. They wouldn't depend on wind power.

Just before leaving Kitty Hawk, Orville and Wilbur collected shells, sand and bottles of seawater to take home to their nieces and nephews.

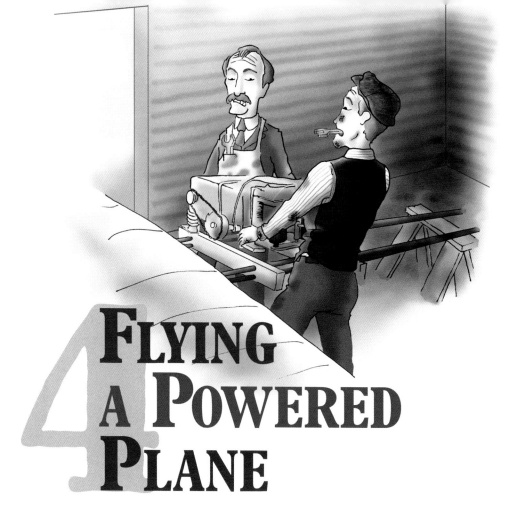

4 FLYING A POWERED PLANE

When they returned to Kitty Hawk in September 1903, Orville and Wilbur took the engine they had built. They bolted it to the plane, called the Flyer. With an engine to turn the two propellers, the plane would lift into the air and fly . . . they hoped!

The Flyer was too heavy to lift off with just the wind. It needed the propellers to start it moving before taking off. The brothers put together a long, straight take-off rail in the sand. Bicycle wheels would guide the aircraft along the rail.

When Orville and Wilbur tested the engine, it rattled and puffed clouds of smoke. The propellers cracked. Then the brothers had problems with the fuel line. Everything took weeks to repair. During another test, a propeller cracked again. Orville hurried home to Dayton to make stronger propellers.

The Wright brothers built a twelve horsepower, petrol engine to power their Flyer.

By Sunday 13 December Orville was back. The plane was ready. Even the weather was perfect, but the Wright brothers read and walked on the beach. They had promised their father they would never fly on Sundays. On Monday the winds had died down.

Then on the icy cold morning of Thursday 17 December 1903, the winds picked up again. It was Orville's turn. The two brothers clasped hands. Then Orville lay on the lower wing.

Standing by the Wright brothers' camp, the Flyer had a twelve metre wingspan and weighed about 320 kilograms.

The Flyer took off at 10.35 am. Winds rocked the plane, and Orville had a hard time controlling it.

The engine clattered and shook. The propellers turned. The aircraft rattled down the track. It lifted off and climbed. It flew!

When the Flyer landed on the sand, the plane had flown under its own power for twelve seconds and gone 35 metres. It was the world's first powered, controlled flight.

Next, Wilbur flew the Flyer for a fifteen-second flight. Orville took another turn. On the fourth flight, Wilbur was in the air for fifty-nine seconds. It was time for the brothers to celebrate.

They telegraphed their father and sister. 'Successful four flights Thursday morning. . . . Inform Press home Christmas.'

WITNESSING THE FIRST FLIGHT

The brothers raised a small flag above the work shed. It was a signal that a powered flight was about to be attempted. Everyone was invited to watch. Orville and Wilbur wanted witnesses. Five men, two boys and a dog watched on 14 December 1903, when the Flyer lifted off the ground for only three and a half seconds. Five witnesses showed up on 17 December 1903. After the flight, one man dashed to the post office in Kitty Hawk. '[Darned] if they ain't flew!' he said.

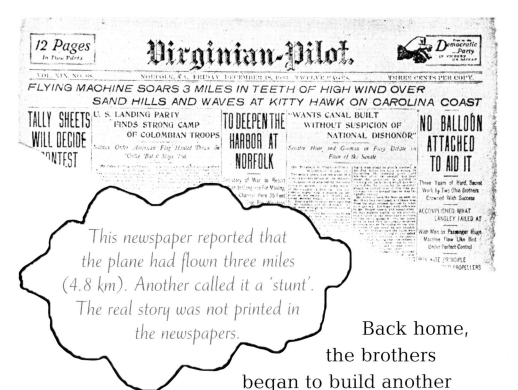

12 Pages
In Two Parts

Virginian-Pilot.

Democratic
...Party
IN VICTORY
OR DEFEAT

VOL. XIX. NO. 68. NORFOLK, VA., FRIDAY DECEMBER 18, 1903 TWELVE PAGES. THREE CENTS PER COPY.

**FLYING MACHINE SOARS 3 MILES IN TEETH OF HIGH WIND OVER
SAND HILLS AND WAVES AT KITTY HAWK ON CAROLINA COAST**

**TALLY SHEETS
WILL DECIDE
CONTEST**

U. S. LANDING PARTY
FINDS STRONG CAMP
OF COLOMBIAN TROOPS

**TO DEEPEN THE
HARBOR AT
NORFOLK**

"WANTS CANAL BUILT
WITHOUT SUSPICION OF
NATIONAL DISHONOR"

**NO BALLOON
ATTACHED
TO AID IT**

This newspaper reported that the plane had flown three miles (4.8 km). Another called it a 'stunt'. The real story was not printed in the newspapers.

Back home, the brothers began to build another plane. At Huffman Prairie, north-east of Dayton, the brothers flew first one new and improved Flyer, then the next. Still, there were crashes. Wilbur and Orville kept iodine and bandages handy for grazes and bruises.

Over the next two years, the brothers built a plane that could fly to the end of a field, turn, come back and then land safely. On 5 October 1905 Wilbur flew *Flyer III* for over thirty minutes. He covered thirty-eight kilometres before the plane ran out of petrol.

Sometimes people came out from Dayton to watch Wilbur and Orville. When newspaper reporters turned up, the weather was often bad or the plane wouldn't fly properly. So Orville and Wilbur never made headlines, except when they did something wrong. Tired of being called names, they decided to show the world what they had really accomplished.

Soaring above Huffman Prairie, the FLYER III was essentially the world's first practical aeroplane.

5 FAME

On 8 August 1908, Wilbur flew their new Flyer in France. A huge crowd watched. Newspapers went wild over 'the great white bird'. France went crazy over Wilbur. Everyone wanted a green racing driver's cap just like Wilbur's.

Wilbur flies the 1908 Flyer over horse-drawn carriages in France.

In September Orville flew the newest Flyer at Fort Myer, Virginia. After seeing one flight, reporters and army personnel were stunned. Orville Wright was really flying!

Wilbur kept flying in France, breaking record after record. Later, Orville and Katharine joined him. The brothers were famous.

When they returned to Dayton in May 1909 thousands of people greeted them. Marching bands, festivities and fireworks were part of the day. A carriage and four white horses carried them home. Flags and banners decorated the house.

Shy Wilbur and Orville didn't enjoy all the attention, but it was only the beginning. In the autumn of 1909, Wilbur flew along the Hudson River in New York City. More than one million people watched his thirty-three-minute flight.

Dayton, Ohio, welcomes the Wright brothers home with a huge celebration. It included a 'flag' of school-children dressed in red, white and blue.

Orville, Katharine, and Wilbur (LEFT TO RIGHT), on board a ship.

The brothers formed the Wright Company on 22 November 1909. Wilbur was president. Orville was vice president. They did not have to repair bicycles anymore. They were rich. Countries were buying their planes and paying them for advice. In February 1912, they bought land overlooking Dayton. Orville and an architect began to design a mansion. It was named Hawthorn Hill.

The house was being built when Wilbur fell ill. He had a disease called typhoid fever. He became more and more ill.

Wilbur died on 30 May 1912, at the age of forty-five. Newspapers around the world wrote about Wilbur's death. The family received thousands of sympathy telegrams and a train carriage full of flowers.

Orville lost interest in work. He played with his nieces and nephews and took them on trips. Orville, Katharine and their father moved into Hawthorn Hill in 1914.

Later that summer the First World War began in Europe. Orville hoped that planes would be used only to watch for the enemy on the ground, but they were also used to fight. Orville believed that war was terrible.

Orville, Bishop Wright, Katharine and some of their relatives sit on the lawn at Hawthorn Hill.

With Wilbur gone, Orville's heart wasn't in the aeroplane business and he sold the Wright Company. Orville was still interested in inventions and tinkered in a laboratory he built at Hawthorn Hill.

When the war ended in 1918, President Woodrow Wilson appointed Orville to the National Advisory Committee for Aeronautics. This committee looked for ways to improve flight. One of the members was Charles Lindbergh. He and Orville became close friends.

CHARLES LINDBERGH

There were many other heroes in the sky. One was Charles Lindbergh, who in 1927 was the first person to fly solo across the Atlantic Ocean. He flew non-stop from New York to Paris, France. A Wright motor powered his plane, the SPIRIT OF ST LOUIS. Crowds followed Lindbergh wherever he went, even when he stopped in Dayton, Ohio, to visit his friend Orville Wright.

Orville tinkers with a small motor.

Orville still loved tinkering. He built a clothes-rinsing machine, a toaster and a stove. He was tinkering with a doorbell on 27 January 1948 when he had a heart attack. He died three days later at the age of seventy-six.

Orville and Wilbur had shared the same dreams. Their aeroplane changed the world. Yet Orville had said, 'I got more thrill out of flying before I had ever been in the air at all – while lying in bed thinking how exciting it would be to fly.'

TIMELINE

In the year . . .

1893   the Wright brothers opened a bicycle shop.

1899   Wilbur discovered wing-warping.
The Wright brothers built and flew a glider.   Age 32

1900   they tested their 1900 glider at Kitty Hawk,
North Carolina, in September and October.

1901   they tested their 1901 glider at Kitty Hawk
in July and August.

1902   they tested their 1902 glider at Kitty Hawk in
September and October.
They began to build a motor for their glider.

1903   Orville made the world's first powered   Age 32
flight on 17 December at Kitty Hawk, North
Carolina.

1905   the Wright brothers built the *Flyer III*.

1908   Wilbur flew the *Type A Flyer* in France.
Orville flew the *Type A Flyer* for the Army
Signal Corps in Virginia.

1912   Wilbur Wright died on 30 May.   Age 45

1917   the United States of America entered the
First World War.

1918   the First World War ended.

1920   Orville was appointed a member of the
National Advisory Committee for
Aeronautics.

1932   the Wright Memorial was dedicated at Kitty
Hawk, North Carolina.

1938   the Wright brothers' bicycle shop and
family home were moved to historic
Greenfield Village, Michigan.

1948   Orville died on 30 January.   Age 76
The 1903 Wright Flyer was installed at the
Smithsonian Institution on 17 December.

CONTROLLED FLIGHT

Inventors like Otto Lilienthal and Octave Chanute had worked out how to make wings that flew. Other inventors worked on engines to power flying machines. Only the Wright brothers realized that a pilot would need to control a flying machine in all three axes. These axes are pitch, roll and yaw.

Pitch is the up and down movement of a plane's nose.

Roll is the side-to-side movement of a plane.

Yaw is the side-to-side movement of a plane's nose.

FURTHER READING

Lynch, Emma. *The Wright Brothers* (Lives and Times) Heinemann Library, 2005.

Nahum, Andrew. *Flying Machines* (Eyewitness Guide) Dorling Kindersley Publishers Ltd, 2003.

Oxlade, Chris. *Aeroplanes* (Machines Inside Out) Hodder Wayland, 2008.

Platt, Richard. *Flight* (DK Experience) Dorling Kindersley Publishers Ltd, 2006.

Sheehan, Sean. *From the Wright Brothers to the Treaty of Versailles* (Modern Eras Uncovered). Raintree, 2006.

Tames, Richard. *The Wright Brothers* (Life Times) Franklin Watts Ltd, 2003.

WEBSITES

Wright Brothers Aeroplane Company and Museum of Pioneer Aviation
An amazing cyber-museum of the Wright brothers' life work. Includes many interactive features.

The Wright Brothers – Henry Ford Museum and Greenfield Village
<www.hfmgv.org/exhibits/wright/default.asp>
A tour of the historical village where the Wright brothers' home and bicycle shop now reside.

History of Aviation
http://www.whom.co.uk/squelch/bb_aviate.htm
This website has pictures and information on fifty of the
greatest aircraft in history.

SELECT BIBLIOGRAPHY

Crouch, Tom. *The Bishop's Boys: A Life of Wilbur and
Orville Wright.* New York: W W Norton, 1989.

Crouch, Tom. 'On Wheels and Wings.' In *Inventors and
Discoverers,* edited by Elizabeth Newhouse. Washington,
DC: The National Geographic Society, 1988.

Culick, Fred E C and Spencer Dunmore. *On Great White
Wings: The Wright Brothers and the Race for Flight.* New
York: Hyperion, 2001.

Freedman, Russell. *The Wright Brothers: How They
Invented the Airplane.* New York: Holiday House, 1991.

Howard, Fred. *Wilbur and Orville: A Biography of the
Wright Brothers.* New York: Alfred A Knopf, 1987.

INDEX

Acknowledgements

For photographs and artwork: © Bettmann/CORBIS, pp 4, 24, 35, 39, 40, 43; Library of Congress, pp 7, 10, 11, 14, 15, 19, 23, 25, 31, 32, 33, 36, 38, 41; From the Collections of Henry Ford Museum and Greenfield Village, pp 8, 9; © Hulton-Deutsch Collection/CORBIS, pp 16, 27; American Heritage Center, University of Wyoming, p 18; Laura Westlund, p 20; © CORBIS, p 28.
Front cover (both), Travel Information Division, Department of Conservation and Development, Raleigh, NC. **Back cover**, © Bettmann/CORBIS.
For quoted material: pp 13, 23, Marvin K. McFarland, editor, *The Papers of Wilbur and Orville Wright* (New York: McGraw-Hill, 1953, 2001); pp 15, 19, Ivonette Wright Miller, compiler, *Wright Reminiscences* (Dayton, OH: Privately printed, 1978); pp 17, 34 (sidebar), Fred E C Culick and Spencer Dunmore, *On Great White Wings: The Wright Brothers and the Race for Flight* (New York: Hyperion, 2001); pp 24, 28, Russell Freedman, *The Wright Brothers: How They Invented the Airplane* (New York: Holiday House, 1991); p 34, telegram to Bishop Wright from Orville Wright, December 17, 1903; p 37, Tom D Crouch, *The Bishop's Boys: A Life of Wilbur and Orville Wright* (New York: W. W. Norton & Company, 1989); p 43, Orville Wright, *How We Invented the Airplane: An Illustrated History*. edited by Fred C Kelly (New York: Dover Publications, 1983).